Destined To Break The Curse Devotional

by Sean Smith, Sr.

J Merrill Publishing, Inc., 434 Hillpine Dr., Columbus, OH 43207 USA.
© 2019 J Merrill Publishing, Inc

Table of Contents

1 - I AM MORE THAN A CONQUEROR 1

2 - I AM NOT A FAILURE (I MAY HAVE FAILED BUT IT'S NOT FINAL) 7

3 - I AM AN OVERCOMER 13

4 - I AM NOT A PRODUCT OF MY PAST 19

5 - I AM LOVED 25

6 - I AM WALKING INTO MY PURPOSE 31

7 - I CHOOSE TO FORGIVE 37

8 - I SHALL DESTROY THE YOKE OF FEAR 43

9 - I SHALL DESTROY THE YOKE OF DISCOURAGEMENT 49

10 - I SHALL NOT GIVE UP 55

11 - I SHALL LEAD MY FAMILY INTO VICTORY 61

12 - I SHALL DESTROY ALL DEMONIC ACCESS TO ME 67

What is a declaration?

dec·la·ra·tion

/ˌdeklərāSH(ə)n/

noun

formal or explicit statement or announcement.

The purpose of this book is to give 12 declarations along with scriptural context to help you grow spiritually and destroy every yoke attached to your life. In reading these 12 declarations and scriptures throughout the year I pray your faith grows to another level. I also pray that you begin to understand why God loves you and the sacrifice He made because of that love. You are special to Him and He wants to heal every broken place you may have within you. With each Declaration I pray strength arise, hope arise and peace becomes a part of your life. With each Scripture I pray the Word becomes nourishment to your soul and plants seeds for you to grow. I pray that you fully step into the promises of God that are over your life.

REMEMBER

YOU ARE DESTINED TO BREAK THE CURSE

1 - I AM MORE THAN A CONQUEROR

YOU HAVE THE ABILITY TO CONQUER EVERY TASK AND EVERY ADVERSE SITUATION. WITH CHRIST YOU CAN DO ANYTHING AND THROUGH CHRIST YOU ARE MORE THAN A CONQUEROR. A CONQUEROR IS AN INDIVIDUAL, OR PEOPLE, WHO HAVE FORCEFULLY TAKEN CONTROL OF A PARTICULAR REGION OR AREA. WITH CHRIST IN YOU, YOU ARE MORE THAN THAT.

EVERY MORNING DECREE INTO THE ATMOSPHERE THAT YOU ARE VICTORIOUS OVER EVERYTHING THAT MAY COME YOUR WAY.

Personal Declaration(s)

Romans 8:37-39 King James Version (KJV) 37 Nay, in all these things we are more than conquerors through him that loved us. 38 For I am persuaded, that neither death, nor life, nor angels, nor principalities, nor powers, nor things present, nor things to come, 39 Nor height, nor depth, nor any other creature, shall be able to separate us from the love of God, which is in Christ Jesus our Lord

Reflection Scripture(s)

2 - I AM NOT A FAILURE (I may have failed but it's not final)

YOU MAY HAVE FAILED BUT IT IS NOT FINAL. IN LIFE THERE ARE CONSISTENT UPS AND DOWNS. IN MAY OF 2018 I HAD A STROKE. MY ALIGNMENT WITH MY LEFT SIDE. MY FACE WAS CROOKED, MY ARM WAS MESSED UP AND I FELT LIKE I WAS GOING TO DIE. GOD SUPERNATURALLY HEALED ME WHILE I WAS IN THE HOSPITAL. IN JUNE OF 2018 I GO TO HAVE A CHECK UP AND TAKE A FEW TEST AND THE WORST THING IMAGINABLE HAPPENED. I DIED ON THE TABLE TAKING THE TEST. I WAS HOOKED UP TO A HEART RATE MACHINE THE ENTIRE TIME. I CAN REMEMBER LOOKING AT THE LINE GO UP AND DOWN CONTINUOUSLY. THE DOCTOR SHOWED ME PROOF THAT I DIED AND THE PROOF WAS THE LINE DIDN'T GO UP AND DOWN BUT IT WAS FLAT. WHAT IM SAYING IS... LIFE IS TRULY FULL OF MOMENTS YOU FEEL DOWN BUT YOU HAVE INSIDE OF YOU THE ABILITY TO GET BACK UP EVERY TIME. GOD ULTIMATELY HAS THE FINAL SAY AND AS YOU LIVE FOR HIM HE WILL CONSISTENTLY HELP YOU GET UP EVERY TIME.

Personal Declaration(s)

Proverbs 24:16 The godly may trip seven times, but they will get up again. But one disaster is enough to overthrow the wicked

Reflection Scripture(s)

3 - I AM AN OVERCOMER

WHAT, AND WHO, IS INSIDE OF YOU HAS GIVEN YOU THE POWER AND AUTHORITY TO OVERCOME WHAT MAY HAVE ATTEMPTED TO OVERCOME YOU. UNDERSTAND THAT YOU ARE A CHILD OF GOD, A ROYAL PRIESTHOOD, A PECULIAR PEOPLE WHO HAS BEEN CHOSEN, BY THE LORD, TO DO GREAT THINGS. IT IS CHRIST INSIDE OF YOU THAT GIVES YOU THE POWER TO FIGHT AND WIN!

Personal Declaration(s)

John 4:4 You are from God, little children, and have overcome them; because greater is He who is in you than he who is in the world.

Reflection Scripture(s)

4 - I AM NOT A PRODUCT OF MY PAST

TRUE REPENTANCE IS WHEN A PERSON CONFESSES EVERYTHING THEY HAVE DONE TO GOD AND ASKS GOD TO FORGIVE THEM. NOT ONLY ARE THEY LAYING IT ALL OUT. THEY ARE ESTABLISHING A COMMITMENT AND A LAW IN THEIR OWN HEART NOT TO DO THOSE THINGS AGAIN. THE DECISIONS YOU MADE IN THE PAST DO NOT, CAN NOT AND WILL NOT DETERMINE WHAT GOD DOES WITH YOU, AS LONG AS YOU REPENT. SO STOP FOCUSING ON THE MISTAKES AND BEGIN FOCUSING ON THE PROMISES.

Personal Declaration(s)

Philippians 3:13-14 13 Brethren, I count not myself to have apprehended: but this one thing I do, forgetting those things which are behind, and reaching forth unto those things which are before, 14 I press toward the mark for the prize of the high calling of God in Christ Jesus.

Reflection Scripture(s)

5 - I AM LOVED

AT TIMES, YOUR MIND WILL HAVE YOU THINKING THAT NOBODY IS THERE, NOBODY COULD POSSIBLY RELATE TO YOU OR THAT NOBODY CARES ABOUT WHAT YOUR GOING THROUGH. ONE THING FOR CERTAIN AND TWO THINGS FOR SURE...YOU ARE NEVER ALONE. WHEN YOU FEEL LIKE NO ONE IS THERE TO TALK TO, OR COMFORT, YOU IN YOUR TIME OF NEED... LOOK TO GOD. HE HAS ALWAYS BEEN THERE WAITING FOR YOU TO CALL ON HIM. WHEN YOU CALL TRUST THAT HE WILL ANSWER AND HIS ANSWER IS THE ELIMINATION OF THE PROBLEM.

Personal Declaration(s)

1 John 4:9-10 In this was manifested the love of God toward us, because that God sent his only begotten Son into the world, that we might live through him. 10 Herein is love, not that we loved God, but that he loved us, and sent his Son to be the propitiation for our sins.

Reflection Scripture(s)

6 - I AM WALKING INTO MY PURPOSE

THERE IS A PLAN FOR YOUR LIFE. LEARNING YOUR IDENTITY IN CHRIST RELEASES THE REVELATION OF YOUR PURPOSE. KNOW THAT IN THE EYES OF OUR CREATOR YOU ARE UNIQUE AND SPECIAL. YOU ARE CREATED TO BE GREAT, PREDESTINED TO WIN YOU WILL NOT FAIL!

Personal Declaration(s)

Ephesians 2:10 For we are God's masterpiece. He has created us anew in Christ Jesus, so we can do the good things he planned for us long ago.

Reflection Scripture(s)

7 - I CHOOSE TO FORGIVE

TRUE REPENTANCE MEANS TO GO 180 DEGREES THE OTHER WAY. TO TURN FROM ALL WICKEDNESS AND DO WHAT CHRIST HAS CALLED YOU TO DO. BUT, IF YOU DO NOT FORGIVE OTHERS, EVEN IF THEY DO NOT ASK FOR FORGIVENESS, YOU CANNOT EXPECT GOD TO FORGIVE YOU. FORGIVENESS FREES YOU FROM THE BONDAGE UNFORGIVENESS TANGLES YOU UP IN.

Personal Declaration(s)

Matthew 6:14-15 "For if ye forgive men their trespasses, your heavenly Father will also forgive you: But if ye forgive not men their trespasses, neither will your Father forgive your trespasses."

Matthew 5:23-24 So if you are about to offer your gift to God at the altar and there you remember that your brother has something against you, leave your gift there in front of the altar, go at once and make peace with your brother, and then come back and offer your gift to God.

Reflection Scripture(s)

8 - I SHALL DESTROY THE YOKE OF FEAR

WHEN YOU KNOW THAT THE LORD IS WITH YOU AND HE LIVES INSIDE OF YOU FEAR IS NOT AN OPTION. THE LORD INSIDE YOU MEANS HE IS WITH YOU, WALKING WITH YOU THROUGHOUT EVERYTHING YOU MAY DEAL WITH. EVERY STEP OF YOUR DAY IS A STEP INTO DESTINY. THE HOLY GHOST AND FEAR CANNOT RESIDE IN THE SAME ENVIRONMENT SO, IF GOD IS IN YOU, FEAR DOES NOT HAVE LEGAL ACCESS TO REMAIN THERE.

Personal Declaration(s)

Isaiah 41:10 Fear thou not; for I am with thee: be not dismayed; for I am thy God: I will strengthen thee; yea, I will help thee; yea, I will uphold thee with the right hand of my righteousness.

Reflection Scripture(s)

9 - I SHALL DESTROY THE YOKE OF DISCOURAGEMENT

DISCOURAGEMENT AND FEAR ARE NOT ALLOWED TO RESIDE IN THE BODY OF A FAITH FILLED BELIEVER. NO LONGER ARE YOU GOING TO BE HELD CAPTIVE BY WHAT DOESN'T BELONG TO YOU. DISCOURAGEMENT DOESN'T BELONG TO YOU. YOU ARE ABLE TO DO WHATEVER GOD HAS PLACED IN YOUR HEART TO DO. YOU HAVE BEEN PREDESTINED TO WALK IN PURPOSE, ON PURPOSE WITH PURPOSE.

Personal Declaration(s)

Deuteronomy 31:8 The LORD himself goes before you and will be with you; he will never leave you nor forsake you. Do not be afraid; do not be discouraged

Reflection Scripture(s)

10 - I SHALL NOT GIVE UP

A DAY IS COMING WHERE YOU WILL BE REWARDED FOR ALL YOU HAVE DONE. YOU HAVE CHRIST ON THE INSIDE OF YOU AND HE GIVES YOU THE STRENGTH TO KEEP GOING WITHOUT FAILING. YOU WILL OBTAIN YOUR GOALS. YOU WILL WALK IN YOUR PROMISES. YOU WILL BE WHO GOD CREATED YOU TO BE. THE STRENGTH THAT IS WITHIN YOU COMES FROM BUILDING A PERSONAL ALTAR... A PERSONAL RELATIONSHIP WITH JESUS CHRIST. GET READY TO GAIN ACCESS TO YOUR DESTINY!

Personal Declaration(s)

2 Chronicles 15:7-8 Be ye strong therefore, and let not your hands be weak: for your work shall be rewarded. And when Asa heard these words, and the prophecy of Oded the prophet, he took courage, and put away the abominable idols out of all the land of Judah and Benjamin, and out of the cities which he had taken from mount Ephraim, and renewed the altar of the Lord, that was before the porch of the Lord."

Reflection Scripture(s)

11 - I SHALL LEAD MY FAMILY INTO VICTORY

DAYS WILL COME THAT YOU FEEL AS THOUGH YOU CAN NOT GO ANY FURTHER. THAT FEELING COMES FROM BEING TIRED PHYSICALLY, MENTALLY, OR EMOTIONALLY. WHEN YOU REACH THAT PLACE, CONNECT WITH YOUR FAMILY OR A GROUP OF PEOPLE WHO BELIEVE IN YOUR PURPOSE. BY CONNECTING WITH SOMEONE ELSE YOU ARE ABLE TO SHIFT SOME OF THE WEIGHT YOU ARE EXPERIENCING DURING THE WAIT. THERE TRULY IS STRENGTH IN NUMBERS. GOD WILL GIVE YOU THE ABILITY TO LEAD YOUR FAMILY INTO A PLACE OF PEACE, PROSPERITY AND PROMISE.

Personal Declaration(s)

1 Corinthians 15:57-58 "But thanks be to God, which giveth us the victory through our Lord Jesus Christ. Therefore, my beloved brethren, be ye stedfast, unmoveable, always abounding in the work of the Lord, forasmuch as ye know that your labour is not in vain in the Lord."

Exodus 17:11-13 11 As long as Moses held up his hands, the Israelites were winning, but whenever he lowered his hands, the Amalekites were winning. 12 When Moses' hands grew tired, they took a stone and put it under him and he sat on it. Aaron and Hur held his hands up—one on one side, one on the other—so that his hands remained steady till sunset. 13 So Joshua overcame the Amalekite army with the sword.

Reflection Scripture(s)

12 - I SHALL DESTROY ALL DEMONIC ACCESS TO ME

STOP GIVING UNNECESSARY ACCESS TO THE DEVIL. BEGIN LOOKING AT YOUR LIFE THROUGH A SPIRITUAL LENS. OUR ADVERSARY THE DEVIL WILL DO ANYTHING HE CAN TO ENTER INTO OUR HEARTS AND MINDS. SO, YOU MUST CUT ALL ACCESS OFF! DELIVERANCE WITHOUT FORMING A TRUE RELATIONSHIP WITH JESUS CHRIST AND BEING FILLED WITH THE HOLY GHOST IS EXTREMELY DANGEROUS! IT IS CHRIST ON THE INSIDE ACCOMPANIED BY THE HOLY GHOST THAT LOCKS THE DOORS WITHIN YOU, SO THE DEVIL CANNOT GET BACK IN.

Personal Declaration(s)

Matthew 12:43-45 "When the unclean spirit is gone out of a man, he walketh through dry places, seeking rest, and findeth none. Then he saith, I will return into my house from whence I came out; and when he is come, he findeth it empty, swept, and garnished. Then goeth he, and taketh with himself seven other spirits more wicked than himself, and they enter in and dwell there: and the last state of that man is worse than the first. Even so shall it be also unto this wicked generation."

Ephesians 4:27 "Neither give place to the devil".

Luke 34-35 The light of the body is the eye: therefore when thine eye is single, thy whole body also is full of light; but when thine eye is evil, thy body also is full of darkness. Take heed therefore that the light which is in thee be not darkness."

Reflection Scripture(s)

www.ingramcontent.com/pod-product-compliance
Lightning Source LLC
Chambersburg PA
CBHW020145130526
44591CB00030B/234